I0797493

THIRD
HAND
BOOKS

YOU'RE CALLED BY THE SAME SOUND

Alicia Wright

Thirdhand Books
Logan, Utah
3rdhandbooks.com

Thirdhand Books LLC, Logan, UT 84321
www.3rdhandbooks.com

Printed in the United States of America

Library of Congress Cataloging-in-Publication Data on File

ISBN (paperback): 9781949344660
1 2 3 4 5

Front cover image: An untitled photograph by an unidentified photographer, c. 1945

Cover design by Lindsey Webb.

Contents

I.

Wraparound

I thought that if we let it go—the property—the
daisy field—the dog's small coffin—the osage orange
tree—its second trunk—held up by wood stands—
her seashell tumblers—their fixed gin—the bomb
shelter forty concrete feet—beneath the ground—we'd
be unlocked—no holding pattern—we'd know—
reinvention—I thought in prying—open the square—
structure—less the brickwork—than the formal
bind—the code untouched—the louver doors
—shot through with sun—integrity—slipped asleep—
we'd know—the home unhad is nothing—its shape
of sorrow—& our sunk now—I thought—we'd be
a we—but this despair—has gashed the field—of them
& me—I've since spent—nights circling back—wet-wheeling—
thinning the veneer—that property—the hunted space
—itself is free—I thought in letting go—I'd know—
detachment's sight—the porch ferns' fade—the holly's
flames—I let it go—the house's routes—how we—
once loved each other—for a while when I—belonged—
how can I let—what I habit—the dimming light—
the room wherein—she died I died—& though I go—
its world in keep—my sorrow slung—I thought one—
living structure'd—last—alcove decay—the opened
door & here the—the pond's—pooling—I come
dipped in—the washtub where—their hands bathed me—

Town Under Lake

Cooper Furnace Ruins, Lake Allatoona, Georgia

Can one tell by passing by
spring grown lake contained dish lake
either alluvial clay

I can with this water but I know
chimney remnant pig-iron Cooper furnace
limestone fracturing

What has been done with a landscape
built over, razed in warfire sunk ethics & bonds
vested interests

Of the destroyed Etowah not the first
Etowah: as distinct, still distinct in native mounds
stolen name sounds

I won't rebuild its story, ankle-deep
in that site, village, skeleton though it asks it of me, industrial
bankrupted, disused

Pulsing lens, see me floating
in the loamy lake snorkeling with my father
underwater foundation

of a house called Glen Holly
what have we done with this dead town but swim in it, imminent
domain, dammed-in

Brushing silt off porcelain, my fingers trail
    small clouds: nails, ore, split   bricks my father & I pile up
                    infected fragments

We are in the lake into sundown
    & hear the rumored spirit horn   over insect chirr, railroad spikes
                    ghost-blown at dusk

By the man shot in the head
    by a minié ball & lived   in a charred, fallen house
                    unsound ancestry

When we come here we hear it
    I have so many handfuls   of shadows looking
                    backward ten degrees

What does it mean to submerge into
    extant truth: a rippling hell   logging sites, a brutal forge
                    factory's currency

To see pieces scattered & know
    that inbuilt system   names unfound & out of water
                    one's own face

In finding that the town is all around
    now Allatoona, lake of subsuming   I'll be your weir
                    held into reckoning

Cloud of Unknowing

I look for it always, the thick, vespertine gloaming that douses the day's heat.
—Sally Mann, *Deep South* (2005)

I.

dart the longing love the love in, the love of

surrender *Pain* the European philosopher

& the photographer conclude

the South has it, the rest of the United States does not—

that *lingering aftertaste*

and the Europeans *feel so oddly at home*

the blue-sensitive film

phenomena: soft and vague

deployed: we see the same tree: that light

only lights what flashes back

capping light, white crests the eye dart

dark longing sea that light we don't

all live under the same burning energy what of

dark matter humming between particles

sorrow *honor* *graciousness*

The tread of the occupier's boot—The South has

known *The South has it* *the rest*

of the United States does

rural denial

unseen occupations *not*

II.

O specious vision   blinding vespers

massacre of

analogy gloaming over   how

to   make   the song even

deeper: to become *attenuated, weirdly responsive*

in collodion   grows

in flash paper   gun cotton   grows

that dimension of revelation and ecstasy that eludes

historical time   dart what is linear

Bound by oak-netting over   that vanishing

point to   via negativa

I have marked my way   through a cloud of

forgetting   I   have worn

garments gloam-soaked   darted the longing

for   failed rebellion   self-censure

I have her   image: long-haired child she

stands before the half-burned mill towering

upward her owning ruin out of frame

If there can be any love unlost it would

live in her staring down the lens

Eclipse

Four wood ducks   dip in flight

air arrowing wingtips   I want to ask

my father the word   for the sound of a bullet's arc

toward the ground   burn above

close bend in the ocean of air   permanent lag

It was the sound of the word of his death

Air unto air   the word   night as clear as day

I reach out   and he's not there
                                        my father's grave
was dug by hand, in the rain

hand glides along   his pecan coffin's grain

not a word in my tongue

celestial absence   darkness and light alike

No dark between us
                              but for the light I feel

Night Habit

I have a night habit, darkly moving in air,

Not mattering—a veil of incident light.

Mother-of-pearl field luster, I park inside

A streak of hill cane, where an opening folds

Me in by the perennial stream. I have my night

Habit, see, I am moving in the dark air, no

Matter, no light to veil. I am incident in the

Field, a perennial opening folds me in. Night

Park, lust for pearl. In the front pasture daisies

Diffuse, strands of lucent vapor. I walk over

The hill, a streak of dark. In the field, perennial

Mother in the hollow, I come for my habit—

Air veil, enfold me where I matter, the opening

Dark, the want in me lustering. Over daisies I pearl

A stream of incidents, me stranded with night,

Made hollow by opening, field matter, stranger.

Eclogue with Daylilies

VOICE

But now you ask me, what am I to think of this myself?
Enough, then, enough. Have instead the daylilies in our field
starring curvilinear, their orange mouths' awe. Have the barn
once raised for me, now in decay, that finds itself still wood.
Do you see what I see? Do you know how you desire me?

VOICE

Yes, I know that I am hearing you, but this is both possible
and not possible. I can't touch all that I've sensed in this
dream space. I can never remember your words after you
have left. This seems to be the problem of your messages—
I'm still stuck here in the waiting daisies.

VOICE

This is darkness, simple as nothing that I can't answer.
You can know, though I am not telling you because it must be
known. You generate your flower-thought and recollect your flood.
The landscape you are left with is pocked with battles of all kinds,
is threaded together by their thoughts you can't unthink.

VOICE

The distance I feel between us is unthinkable, as you are the guide
behind the cloud, what I think to be the cloud, what I reach back
and grasp as all my error, all that I've let down, how I can nearly
sense your face through the stinging vapor which I can't feel
on my face but know. Give me yourself locatable, light-touched.
Press through the guise of time; rupture the case of bodied words.

VOICE

Pierce your longing with your longing. You know I won't come
to you any other way. Like you, I am brought to it when I am

asked. I am not a body, I am not a thing to be grasped by thought. If I say cast it all down, then set it down. If you've found your charge, if you can compress it all into a single dart, then make it and relinquish. Keep your love upward.

Historical Eye

I hold
open the

horse's eye
its lids

lip slick
dirt amulet

finger pry
forceps

opening
wider its

fissure I
rip tunics

history's blue
buckskin

I object in
monocular

vision hold
pierce light

tear canthus
the horse's

eye glows
impassive

I form
as opener

held in its
beast gloss

I fasten his
fascination

it pins
me holding

for as
long

as I can
think

II.

Human Bone, Worn Lyre

St. Augustine, Florida

Sunk whole   in flesh   still

in a moment   water air   still

animate   still   currented

femur curve   backbone link

Is it empty   the water touch   it

is dark & falls   away   white   to

black   shift   water   cinder   at

wave's touch   pieces   pressure

curve   spine canal   brush uplift

dredged   path   dredged   to

sand trace   my hand   in shore

I heard it shaped in
thought I heard
it in the hand I heard
it reencountered
in the sound between

the hearers on the
beach up in the
mouth collected in
the hand forgotten
place I heard
a self among the
upswelled things
myself a fossil out of
air

Sotweed Factor Danse Macabre

after *The Sotweed Factor, or A Voyage to Maryland, A Satyr*
by Ebenezier Cooke (1708)

in the arms of the hated nuptial bed

king's world I draw you out you into new

nocturnal riot come fled planter take my hand

corn feeding swine invisible angels must

contract counter imbibing aromatic fire-cure

Peasant: I had to work very much and very hard

from my hands seep apatite my body field trial

anatomy of a landscape sucked lung tar stain

Memento: summon fox snake pig dog sow etc

mori: trepanning to be in golden slumber's best

who was the fool who was the wise man

I can give in stuff my ears with cotten avoid deaf

blue linen of planters rabble beat down bodies blued

after stolen hominy radicles working into vomit rivulet

Fear death   drumming   drumming   in death   these leaves

having to believe   just as pink flowers   onto soil sprayed

the equalizing   crop   to be topped

Aceldama

Burning being gathering mass   a man on horseback   low flung meteor
borne down with purpose   unfurling over the ridge   God's anonymous muscle
moonless shadow   denser than his horse's vessels   tremor and contract
under intent, no step his own   divinely guided between outposts
If a man has no land   he might still possess   the words of the father
which spread with him   imagining bread as ashes   giving thanks for his endurance
incarnate state   vesture of wildflowers   here a vast green luxuriant meadow
In his vision beauty that surpasses   springing up in all directions
as much as the eye can take   countlessness, given and adorned   for him
wild strawberries so profuse   his horse's hoofs   staining deep red as they tread
For him, his thought's the seed   himself the lone post oak   each cell a spur
for he's received   that which cannot be exchanged   the word become
his word, alone   portent requiring disbursal   his mission replicates
a dandelion whose detonated head   falls along the conical hill
obliterating coreopsis   like thirty silver pieces   gotten when he lands
a betrayal severing communion   darkest lightning   in the somber belts of timber

Compress Pastoral

for Jude Walters, operator at Rome Cotton Compress Company

Not another one like it for a hundred-odd miles

This cotton compress's so efficient it needs only one operator

No spider men darting around iron legs losing fingers

The oldest one still in operation also owned by the same man

Whose customary reticence shortened threads we have left

Jude who runs the big machine while the owner hunts in Nova Scotia

Selling bale by bale in Boston bale by bale 500 lbs a bale

Stated commission: 50 cents per bale when local sourcing

These bales the preference of the surrounding mills

Prices shift per telegram: 5 1/8, 5 5/8 4s you don't care

Top crop or small fruit which makes the grade

Even disinterested experts confirm the plant's superior

Whether or not the cotton's injured or will have a bad showing

Harbor (meaning wait and do nothing) as spots don't respond

To decline in futures

Jude you are full of care moving under the belly

The machine like a ladder too high to picture with its bell dome

Crushing the cotton you confirmed was of quality not slipping

In shifting gradients these distinctions to you the most clear

Removal Fort

The Trail of Tears, Fort Means, an internment camp near Kingston, Georgia/ᏣᎳᎩᏯᏗᏍ (Cherokee) land, 1838

early budding   of *relocating*   briers needling in fence corners
Means's men monitor the fallow field   the collection point
holding them   467   Fort structure: destroying angel   speaks: *after*
the drum beat should beat, no one must be seen out doors till morning   Captive
under its universal veil   He's deaf   & mute & has tracked
no shift of this   gone-dark meadow   invisible net   approach
If he can never have   his cabin again   what language then
Flagging himself he flees   in the field breaking   not
having heard   the soldier's order   No one can tell him what is
coming   in sprint his limbs flying   *Turn left*   he turns right
If anyone called   out   he'd never   silence granted in him
white-hot   dart radiating   in his body that sound

Surveyor: John Seaborn, 1831

Cass County, Georgia, ᏣᎳᎩᎠᏰᎵ (Cherokee) land

Few others would come by
foot as I have carried Myself
westward over from the
Highlands which so appear
as tho' God him self's right
Hand Figured each hill

There are many pines &
birds are many & bear
signs are many I have only
seen one as it looked me

To do this work I must
picture the world from
above, looking down &
accounting for natural
features there are many
rivers creeks springfed &
which draw such fertile

When I am not holding
to my thoughts the
rectangular system
becomes more particular

As a State Agent I have
found employ & that is
more than any scrub
patch of soil the cotton
plants weak & failing No
one can change God's

It is good work I am one to
lay down the shape of future
I do not often have to think
of fellow man only when I
have need of others' succor
at encampment or to slake

Villages I'll divide so many
One lucky men will have to
himself attain the chief part:
who when his number's
called in a winning Draw
he might bring his wife
& offspring & all else to a
House cleared out & land &

Lots to be lotto'd if a
man has God on his side
his number drawn & the
lot & whatsoever might
be there therefore is his

If I see no one then
no soul is here I am
fearful & most often
alone it is lonely work
Bruno the dog follows

This tract I do not know if
it will be retained as it has
unusual Mounds I know
what they are but not how

plucking blackberries
ones not dry &
scorched as I pass thru

Right angles in a series
of right angles the
theodolite's fine eye is
the sharpest so I am
told, like my rifle with
2 more arms & poise
to plot later on paper

thicket yes & the kettle
air. Townships must
be six miles square per
the old Rules but
nought else present
out here but those
who stay hidden like

I am a cunning man &
I am well matched in
my companion Bruno
like to use his teeth as

Up at the Hightower camp
I such Company tho' few of
Tell of how I caught the
George Took he was
absconding with a woman
he in God's truth was
dismounted and I sprang
upon him the water from his

But these are my First Drafts
& my Footprints as they make
informal lines will not I have
heard in Virginia a horrible
rebellion has taken place & so
I sleep with my gun by my
side. Won't shoot until I get
word of land ahead & if any

Yesterday a young deer
like a lightning bolt
thru the pines nearly
hung itself catching my
steel half-chain at the
neck its hoof caught
the key handle and as
it stumbled I reached

Buckshot

from "Anecdotes and Reminiscences" in *A History of Rome and Floyd County* by George Macruder Battey Jr. (1922)

. . . Mr. Stewart says   deer used to run

wild through   the woods around

Rome in the thirties   and that Jim Ragan

shot one near the Etowah River and

the foot of Third Avenue   about the location

of the John W. Maddox place in front

of the old J. A.   Gammon home spot   Mrs. Robert

used to have   a pet deer

given her by her   father, William   Smith, and she

had seen   deer jump the   fences

while the dogs

chased them.   Her

deer became enraged

on one occasion,

attacked a woman

had to be shot

Photograph: Alice Allgood Cooper On Her Wedding Trip

Trion Factory, Georgia, 1888

I've heard it said humility's the true knowledge
of self, as we are flawed—and as for me, I trembled
like a one-winged bee when I was loosed into
wedlock. Watch my portrait's power to compose—
there's nothing I want more than to languish
in this threshold of not having to explain, that
flush of feeling, pure hush before a name. Awareness
is an intoxicating tool, I find. I have no questions
I can't ask. Here is the wake of wonder: everywhere
I see's my stage, ornate, these heavy claws that grip
the mirror, flower-carved columns, my traveling
gown a spill of textile: my dowry's an industry
I wear on me, folded into white. It flows over
my wicker chair I lean in lightly, as if a throne's
a thing I can lift off from, leave behind. For him
I've darkened doubt out from around my eyes,
grey jasper set in kohl: darting gifts in my trousseau.
For him I willow-bow my spine. My cuts take soundless
root. These dogwood branches on the windowsill—they're
my touch, stemming freshly. In my spell I am suspended,
seamed into soft-drawn letters I've just learned. Is this
the floating feeling when you've come into love?
My world in sweet proportion with another? My right
hand heats in its long kidskin glove, my left hand draws
out slender, bare—the honest wrongdoing, this hand
that you can see, curving toward me.

In My Father's House There Are Many Houses

A hog-killing, a house, a conjecture, a fall

Strung up hoggish
husbandried
  grid's beauty red
organs spring
  tulip
down
in the barn The

man, farmhand
  starts at the crotch

*

Lent violent
soil exhaustion: Edgefield
is a stone house
And my mother
lives there
Uphill from yipping
God's alone
     If the clay
were red any color's
run into the river

*

If in my father's   house's
house's house is then
                          it's a mansion
                     I've been lived in
how can I   go be outside
                          men have shown
it's structured white

                          corrupted light

*

He's
actively acquiring
     hickory
& branch

images   I have no practice
  chaff   loosened

free of grain   flail

minutiae threshing floor

Jane in Starving Time

Jamestown Settlement, Virginia, 1609

We grasp at everything but clasp nothing

but wind. To have had my girlhood
first at sea
& here, in leafy
canopy, silver cedars, oaks &
wailing, owls

& otherwise in timbered dark—

I'm not like them, their island tongues
unraveling in colony's weak net,

vowels slack-jawed with winter's waste,
old words glittering
like the fishes I did cup in pools

left behind by tide.
Water's salt prickling
my lips. Here, like ropes & knots

of guts, like ivy's rash, I'd learned to read

how bodies are susceptible to change:
I grew shadowed
by water's wane, the curled-down corn. My
chest like wild strawberries's sprung,

but barren swamps you could row through
now won't bear the heavy plough.

How like my face
defleshed
in those
hot seconds
after death.
Fresh apprehension, dull cleaver's

lesson—hunger drives the novice hand
that plats my skin like hair,

my brains the fruit of acorn, bright
& bitter boiling out.

No mirror here
for my teeth's air. No answers
but for *all*

our beasts are slewn. My skull's hackmarks
& punctures sing

our settlement's secret song
to itself—the role of a berry

is to bleed in your mouth.

Okefenokee

Cypress knees the pitch root of it
    the note underlying laying   like stink

sulfur blink bone face chert
                back of the head mud
  water silent nostrils   back brine I

& the old form superimposed onto each
              other just below

It & I facing   upward   vascular ascending
  water drifting over   blank for the time being

Circle base swollen drink up from peat as
body becomes fluid   sandy hushes eke

out I floating crossever gradient radials
      accelerant   branchlets scalelike

  If I aerate am then outgrowth
      denuded roots exposed & rotted

hollow over time form is un-underground
  fibrous structure   needs to breathe

into silt the water's shedding   dissolving
                to particulate   clay

Tabulation

from "Tabloid Facts" in *A History of Rome and Floyd County*
by George Macruder Battey Jr. (1922)

Did you know that—John Hume brought
the first bath-tub in Rome, from Charleston,
about 1850? Daniel R. Mitchell owned the first piano?
Coosa Old Town was an Indian village on the Coosa
River near Rome, South Rome side, and was
destroyed on or about Oct. 17, 1793, by Gen. John
Sevier, ancestor of numerous Romans? An erratic
character known to the Cherokee Indians as the
"Widow Fool" operated a ferry in 1819 at the forks
of the Oostanaula and Hightower (Etowah) Rivers?
Miss Eliza Frances Andrews, botanist, has had
her habitat in Rome since 1911? Major Ridge's ferry,
opposite his home on the Oostanaula, was seized in
1835 by a white man named Garrett, who claimed
that Ridge would not run it or let anybody else
run it? Father Ryan, Indiana poet, once visited Rome to
see about the Kane property in New York, and was the
guest of Mrs. Mary Adkins, mother of Wm. H. Adkins?
Thos. A. Wheat, of Ridge Valley, loaded the first ten-inch
Mortar cartridge fired at Fort Sumter in 1861? The Santa
Ana silver service, captured by Houston at the Battle of
San Jacinto, was once the property of Henry Pope at Pope's
Ferry? Heavy guns furnished the Cherokee Artillery
by the Nobles were captured by Gen. Sherman at Resaca?
Rome once had thirteen whiskey saloons? Before
Barney Swimmer and Terrapin, Cherokees were
hung on Broad Street for robbing and murdering Ezekiel
Blatchford (or Braselton), of Hall County, a land
seeker, in 1837, they were allowed to take a last swim

under guard at the forks of the Etowah and the Oostanaula?
Are you saying *you didn't know, you didn't know, how could you have known?* Each glint in river water? How will you atone?
At knowing's nexus while lives are breaking in the dam?

Everything that Rises

One after another the angel of history
Women: rural, 9, 1536, 1547, 1550, the angel of history
1551—52, 1559; in business, 147; and the angel of history
athletics, 245—46, 565; and education the angel of history
266, 1533, 1536—38; and flowers, 340, the angel of history
385; folkways among, 451, 452; per- the angel of history
I can no longer hear the music the angel of history
Singings, all-day **1039—40** the angel of history
Sit-ins: and civil rights movement the angel of history
Southern Literary Messenger, 909, 933, the angel of history
Big Thicket 335, 350, **377** the angel of history
A cast-iron farm bell the angel of history
The bell rust friable the angel of history
In the fricative air between tolls the angel of history
Make a basket of kudzu twines the angel of history
though these forms are less common the angel of history
shoot-the-chutes. We had been in swimming and we had the angel of history
-hibits African, folk, 15th-century, and contemporary the angel of history
art, among other things. The Cottonlandia Museum in the angel of history
648 History and Manners the angel of history
I heard my mother ring the bell for the angel of history
The king snake in the bush a branch painted the angel of history
A dream of the red-and-black snake the angel of history
Around my throat tightening the angel of history
The hoarse boys shouting in the dark street the angel of history
-Nothings captured political office and established nativist the angel of history
Would the angel of history know when memory the angel of history
Father's House [1978] is a grim novel exploring future the angel of history
Let Gaines rest the angel of history
in peace the angel of history
the monograph had been adhered to an the angel of history
1838 copperplate the angel of history

He asked *What about sin* I'd forgotten the angel of history
South that has all but vanished the angel of history
The fracture in the ledger grave marker the angel of history
The dog that bit my father digs in it the angel of history
Most artists in the South have embraced the tenets of the angel of history
what is loosely called modernism the angel of history
Hot knobs of the rooms I cannot enter the angel of history
wreckage upon wreckage the angel of history
What calls from the dead in the flat air the angel of history
That I can hear the angel of history
Mass., and a Norman-style Episcopal church in the south the angel of history
Moth balls and tin in the slat-shelf pantry the angel of history
Collapse in her last kiss the angel of history
Technocolonialism the barbs on the wire the angel of history
ily, 1049; image of, 1492 the angel of history
Bottle trees **495—496** the angel of history
Into the hulls of westward-racing ships the angel of history
went bags of letters desperately calling the angel of history
A tithe purloin'd cankers the whole estate the angel of history
The ledger the fissure the sin of the dog the angel of history
May at his perill further go the angel of history
Clay clods the slippery elm leaf spray the angel of history
386; as symbol, 586; and concurrent the angel of history
Myself no better than the angel of history
The blood from my mouth the angel of history
The fourth escaped into the tall August sugarcane the angel of history

Requiem with Flamingo Flock

Picture roseate necks extending into
                    sun-warmed water, the

red dipping under palmate shadow,
the saw palm's

petiole spines languid bend
                in salt air with

a hundred calls calling interlaced
in reflection—webbed

                feet lifting sand plumes, legs
back-angled, faces

grazing, hooked bill as two palms
                cupped together

then sailing away
   without flapping their wings

*

And just on the horizon there was this huge line of pink

*

In Gaffney, South Carolina, for Mullinax, Inc.,
a ladies' hat design affixed flamingo plumage
in a braid along the rim, a wreath, the
natural curvature of the feathers molded
around the head in a coquettish cap leaving
birds' original skin discarded in sheaths
and the carcasses to eat. A naturalist's 1860 account
describes how when the birds would molt, he
and a hunter waded through the marsh
to take them bulletless, by the hand. Bird by bird, he took
one hundred from the flock to sell their meat.
Let us remember them. Elusive prize,
a colony sighted on a mud flat would often disappear
when hunters would return, their local guides
unable to account for why they'd gone.
A flamingo was killed in or before 1868 by a Captain R. S.
Sheldon, who *worked five or six hours to get it,* who
skinned it and stuffed it, a skill he'd learned
from an Englishman who'd come to Florida before the
Civil War. He wrote, *It is the only flamingo I ever saw*
in Florida. Audubon's account remarks
they usually move in lines. Other enterprising men would
write to him in hints: *The Flamingo is a kind of bird*
that lives in lagoons having a communication
with the sea. By canoe, bateau, by wading shoulder-deep
in alkaline-tinted mangrove mud the men
did pursue the shy, *rose-coloured, scarlet*
birds into the salt flats so deep within the swamps' interior
the names of sites in records slip—likely one island
but possibly another, a river mouth, the salt
lake, the reservoir, the slick embankment downstream by
one mile, to find the secreted flock inhabiting Mud
Lake—twenty-four so-called in-state. Where
are you, wader? Do you know your footing among the water
lilies, beach verbena, buttonbushes? *Phoenocopterus ruber*

pedaling in lagoons, umbrella silhouettes
stock-still on awnings, cotton shirts, straw hats shading red-
dened faces? Profligate flamingos' casino profits—
now they're taking Vegas—they sip fruits
on beaches which, for them, means possibly three partners.
Wild birds! Hunters thought they had *eliminated* them
by twentieth century's start, but Alice found
a mallet uncooperative for the queen's rigged croquet game,
its neck dropped limp before her swing, or strike on
an unending pitch where death's the stake.

*

In the flock, the signals shift—a honk, a swerve of neck, a high-tide plash—
will glide at glimpse, at lightning strike—the sawgrass sears—it saw—they've seen.

*

The ocean of the gulf is slate   the ocean of the gulf is mirror   arrow-legged they
trace their migratory pattern   in clouds   from Cuba (where they nest if they decide
some spring   though our notes   obscure   where they keep   their home) It is
the Key   is Mexico   it is all land that bowls   the gulf's expanse   it is no mystery
but that our   mystery   is why we   will not locate   home from home   & right to rest

*

A neck bends backward for to preen.
        A neck is serpentine, is filter, flute. A beak
is islanded, tangerine to jet-blackened

as each wing-edge. An eye is bigger than
        a brain. Is always golden in a head.
Tongue sifts salty from the clear. Tongue

flicks flickering a hundred times a lick. A
        tongue so sure in a sloped mouth, a thousand
sensing bristles drink the lake. *In*

a disturbance of words within words
        a field is founded, flamingos folded
colony to colony and so unnoted, found—

they are *not mine,* not spoonbills so
        similar and warm in color, mind. More
than they swill this mudded earth, draw

shrimp glow, seed glow, blue-green algae
        glow to color feather. They hear their fledgling's
calling from inside its egg, before its hatch,

and speak it back. They drink, give back
        in particle. Milk made in-throat, seeped
out from mouth, their young's straight

beak alights to careful ladle. How they
        deposit every drop. How this secreted drip,
flush with carotene, depletes its makers, fills

the blank and squawking fledgling up to color,
        red nectar droplets spilling down its head,
blood-close, and is blood from the head.

III.

Eulogy at Headwaters

In the center of the city an interbraid
　　　　a long eddyline milksnake brown
patching sturgeon green muted queen snake
　　　　green in a ripple as the triad of two
rivers meet to make a third called Coosa, you
　　　　live over the river-making as it flows
westward toward Alabama, where it is caught,
　　　　pooled, by power companies, by
General Electric who use the river's weight
　　　　and flow, you see where this current
is taking you, nuclear, this point of critique as
　　　　distinct from elegy, this is supposed
to generate a pastoral which is commonplace
　　　　to know is contaminated, my thinking
depth cannot nearly reach as deep and into
　　　　purpose, instead a murky churn, and
the darters and crappies dissipating as a hand
　　　　or polychlorinated biphenyl furls
into the three rivers in which you'd swim
　　　　gallantly as either way you drink it
what is shifting is polluting you enter polluting
　　　　the polluted river filled diluted rising
past its banks washing out the ground and into
　　　　groundwater which is untrackable
whether coursing above ground or below you
　　　　breathing in historicity insofar as particles
insofar as the supple lyric cannot hold you

Cotton Block

It's the first avenue downtown   it's a barbeque joint husking
the bend by the bridge   it's a filling station   it's white paint
flecking off brick   it's a sidewalk paraded by   the girls
in white dresses grip crisp stems   it's they are wearing it's

standing on bales stacked   five high   it's heavying bolls
blossom into spindle wheels   it's unsung hands   it's upping
branches like flags   it's an empty grocery   it's & Sons it's
a bicycle shop   it's very expensive bicycling   it's cottoning

on   it's a back parking lot   it's a white flag   it's history's glyph
psychic notches   it's I spilled in the backseat   of David's Jeep
it's eighteen   it's first   floodground   it's where all three rivers rise
it's mutual commerce   it's vested labors   it's blind traffic gliding by

the cemetery base   it's bur & locks bulging   into my leaving
it's untended & keeps   growing   it's blanched cement   it's office
supply   it's dry   it's a native promontory paved   it's blood theft
it's flatbed pallets axled   it's steamboats bumping   it's up the river

banks   it's the belts   carriaging the cotton down   it's intact
brick building blocks   it's spokes spooling   it's every bale
rolled up   it's haze steam windows   it's the antique market
I pick through   it's where I've floated over   its distant floods

Undated Incidents Concerning Occupation

Major Ridge Home, Rome, Georgia, ᏣᎳᎫᏪᏘᏱ (Cherokee) land

Surrounding trappers
envied his two-story

white house which holds
the older dogtrot

house & its pine beams
hand-secured

slopes & local lotto
trickling farmers

see his riparian swaths
of soil & his ferry

the current-holding
vessel bank-to-bank

crossing seamless over
known & newer shoals

the self-sustaining
prosper system

the wealthiest non-
citizen they knew

that property's their
treaty mirage

he signed to pitch
his structure's even

negotiation & he
would again

in near annihilation's
lawless air

*

In order for a ferry boat to go from one side
of a river to another. When a movement,
called ferry, ferrying. It is a management of force.
The current comes a nearly constant. Aim
your vessel at the midpoint of the current
and the bank. If the water's momentum's
low, the angle will be less. Flow. If we're
talking big resistance, you'll want to meet
the water hard, head on. What you want
to be's the ideal angle, so right you won't
have to paddle or propel. A few gestural
strokes. It is like holding space in time, on
a vector shot from one thing to another.
You'll be pushed a perfect sideways glide
unless, of course, a flood or dam's released.

*

The lonesome ringing of a ten-year-old
                                        in an empty kitchen

Glass bottles   swallowed tinctures & corrugated
faucets   laminate counter & warped floor

The not-lit backdoor   where some come in
board members   my mother   archaeologists

bustle the old breezeway   unwrapping
the petit fours uncap the Cokes   for a meeting

I wait   the air's heavier here   like on the staircase
with its low copper-soft railing

its uncanny curve up   & a sudden rise
shadows bend around now   greyed fluorescence

Who's been watching   this whole time   who lived
while my forefather grandmother father me   occupy

where had been sold   Who treads in this ceded house
bought & whitewashed   lead in the chest &

swathed in the totality of holding   overlapping
the house's deep memory   I know here's theirs

If my body like a bullet pitched   sent out
I felt my brain bend back   sense the torque

Of their disruption & yet they've stayed
in structure's still   hewn logs interlocked

Hot Blast Furnace

The specular iron ore, England-approved
Denaturing into razors, shovels, bars
Lucent melting in the pyramidal forge
Fused in molten air, limestone stripped
No need for mining, the open seam
Of a surface median, you could approach
The blast by fueling the tuyere's nozzle
Neutrality's noxious torque, the furnace
Continuously burning, functional slag float,
Countercurrent exchanges that mimic
Flows in nature, flow arrangement's terms
Retaining heat dispersed, historical fantasy
Repeatable form that shapes the past,
Each object cast into illusion, everyday
Domestic technology, function, bonds
Requiring tonnage of timber felled, first
The blades for axes, striking trunks, that
Torqued contortion of converting one
Into a mythic other of abstracted labor
What the stillness of potential strikes
In me: I take it up, for whom the bell,
Past sylphic feinting purposelessness
At the forged core of conducting power,
Oceanic death beyond ocean and death
Objects and order for my image made

Latticed wood planks nailed at forty-five degrees
X's proximate to a small hill, yoked slope's momentum
Carts that rolled the coal toward the charring mouth
Excess carbon burnoff in reduction heat alliance
That substance of unimaginable strength of bonded
Compounds fueled by bondage, extractions intertwined
That which is unspeakable, that vision of production
In the provisional zone the aim to kill all feeling for
One's fellow man, yeomen's fences falsely flagging
No structure thereover nailed without enslavement
No house, foundry, mill, or capital not a scourge
The tracks' two steel lines extending mirror-like
Laid crossover tracks of depravity and deprivation
Look in it, look that you might lose your own face

The fetid scorching breath. Speak to it
Into the maw of cursed condition
Along every crumbling river road
Into each warehouse on its banks,
Honeywell, ferryboat, infrared, cinder
Optimum Technological Enterprise
The vestigial economy impervious
To fire, torching virtue, no one
Imagines hell past burning: the field
Of turnrows tracing networked crops
Enterprise, settlement, nullius merged
As Empire Workforce Solutions or
Infinite Commerce's leveraged promise
Rome's long-fingered settlement
Crude iron telos: bars, chains, links
Extractive corporate reposition stocks
Cast into abomination of a bond

Ash Pond-3

The plant plan's for it
to produce steam power
obfuscatory stacks cap
in place sunk expenditure
filed failure to disclose
instability issues the plan he
said it has a lot of moving
parts per dewatering AP-3
hole the water brownlit
pit & clouded as if fouled
what's kept wet's what
can't breathed or better
yet believed I saw slow
alielluminated flow take
hypotensive knout cuprous
slip coattail can't touched
eventually carp initiative
I don't see my mussel
shells that I used to see
on the sand I don't hear
the frogs at night singed
if what's burned that doe
sn't rise if ash rises as
incinerated flocculant
compensatory question
of the ash dead plant
matter answer the decay
then decommission culm
air deep scintilla burial to
laek a leak esophageal grack
millefleur a farmer's lung
the plan to use an anything
the does or doesn't move

Triolet for the Tumor

after *Battey's Operation, 1872,* a photograph in the Rome Area History Museum

The girl is shown the image by the museum curator.
          He will force the evidence, certain of its puncture, of a body
gone bulbous, doubled, author of a sagging tumor.
          The girl is shown the image by the curator.
The woman stares at her stretched belly carried in a wheelbarrow
          & the uncertain surgeon snips into the world's first oophorectomy.
The girl is shown the image by the curator.
          He will force the evidence of her body, certain of its puncture.

Irradiation

I.

The cotton broker could afford 100 grams of radium,
which he purchased, in consultation with his doctor,
in the summer of 1919. Two facilities produced a quantity
enough to be considered for philanthropic acquisition:
one in Pittsburgh, another Denver. Because the one
out west was cheaper, perhaps speculatively, the broker
placed his order there. It arrived to Rome's medical clinic
intended for the treatment of those who could not
otherwise afford it. Some side effects were beginning
to be charted: laceration, reddening of skin, small burns,
deterioration & weakness overall, but the cotton broker
pressed his business. The cotton broker named himself,
a record shows, a capitalist, & in Boston mediated sales of bales
grown from the upland soil tilled by pennied Reconstruction
labor. He was compensated handsomely. He built schools.
He upheld codes. He owned a textile mill himself, through
his wife's family's tragedy: one brother shot a fiancé, but
that's another angle—a mark way down a barrel. Or is it, as
the deep therapy X-ray machine the broker bought for the
emanation of irradiate luminous metal into superficial
dermis shows otherwise developing cells, discolorations, protrusions,
tumors? The excrescence of a body willed mysteriously away.
The X-ray is a vehicle for sight into tissue, for secrets kept
by bodies until cut, or split, whose cracks or seepages would
self-expire. They activated radium into an idea so they'd contact
the insides of themselves, & blast through killing parts.

II.

The results reported back to the broker justified expense:
During the month of March, we had nine cases for Radium. These cases,

with one exception, were small localized carcinomas, which
usually respond quite readily to Radium treatment, and several

of these have disappeared already. One was an extensive carcinoma
of the breast in which Radium was post-operative, and in which

operation itself would not have been attempted, had not possessed
Radium to follow it up. Four were carcinomas about the head and face

in which surgical measures would have been impossible and where
the only relief lay in the use of Radium. The doctor, cautious

with the application of his source, the Radium Fund, added
on, appreciatively: *You may be interested to know that one of the*

first cases upon which we used the Radium, in a fibroid tumor, returned
several days ago and the tumor has entirely disappeared.

III.

The broker & the doctor understood each other, understood

the fragility & impact, the work of *local use*. Two knowledge
systems overlay, begin to blur to one action: a funded fund,

a store of possibility. The possibility itself makes bodies glow,
brains glow imagining their work: direct a tube conducting
voltage, at low wattage—& point the brain toward the body, watch,

no, feel the work begin. The necessary burning through, though
internal tumors could not be reached without irrecoverable sear,
& if the X-ray's effects were not enough, poison radium drops beading
from a metal tube tip would be touched to tumor, to affected area.

The capital of skin condensed by their formal dialogue. The capital
of who's attritional—some bodies, say the blasting tubes, inflaming
brains, are to be seen in terms of use, disuse. Languages of care
& capital mutate, brokering, raying out from the limits of what
could be known, of what the two men could & would be willing

to be shown. The story here is not an elegy, attending to a death,
though some patients did die despite treatment: *Dead, four; cured,
twenty-six; under treatment, twenty-four; and hopeless, seven,* wrote the
doctor some months later. *There are quite a number of these who are
now under treatment who I feel sure we will be able to transfer to the group
of cured. Those which I have classified as hopeless are ones which presented*

*an impossible condition when they first came and for whom we used
the radium with the hope of relief.* What grows from living bodies
helps us measure distance? What then when a body's dead?
Care's capital displaced into outcome, professionally detached—
how if we care to determine good from bad, bad from worse,

& good from better shapes into, from history's lens, narrative
abscesses. From external beam what can be seen, which samples

ought be held to light? Letters & accounts come radiating selves—
embodied resonance—through contact, brought to sight, illumined
structures, the damage in material, a body's segment layered into shapes
& scanned for meaning. To look at someone like a ray. To see
their body stark, backlit, holding self, curvatures of messages extended,
how healing is a silhouette of power in technology applied
to voices—past this half life each one a separate sound, a sanctity.
Through laying self aside, can work work its way to heal or recombine?

The question's if these, such forms, have been, could be benign.

Origin Story

with lines from George Oppen

Once once only in the deluge Joyride night
was the time I saw unthinkable speed dash

by I didn't blink so trained was I to the crest
of the hill for headlights crouched raccoon

behind the yew bush skintight cropped cami I
had chosen I hadn't eaten this was a normal

This is my only story The plan was to wait
I was wearing black we know what I meant

The light the blur sped around the corner a
freed contrail sprinting on the pavement an

animated fog body whipped around the bend
though I'd once beaten you in a footrace this

has nothing to do with what I saw I was faster
I was waiting for you you were riding for me

Does what I saw hold any meaning for what
I'd do He'd stolen the car We'd unbuckled we'd

unbelted the backseat We broke the warehouse
code For four fourteen-year-olds *if our story shall*

end untold to whom and to what are we ancestral this
is anything What I saw that night what I felt

was a boy body unsure on me   as what I'd seen
Danny we were spiderlings   I never told you

why we could not ever   though you knew and
I had seen what I'd seen that colorless specter

Never Lived in the City

except if you count sprawl ululating & the molar strips of kennels
terraces many mouthed houses & the jacked-up trucks & creeks

trickling embankment runoff kids do that they run loose in cities
trailing after rock straight shot freeway my friend Hilary shows me

no less than ninety in this lane miasmic dense the highway rate swerve
wrecks & down in rabbit holes in little five points the city'd been

granaries   mill houses   block built   affluent   incineration just
the open grit slathered babe as a baby been brought away from

this city later sucked off accent we smoke pig butts & we cannot
lie houses low-level brick porticos kitchenettes & Formica wrought

garden fences the burnt rust underside magnolia leaves like pollen
& Bradford Pears legions emitting dead-fish stink in spring lining

tennis courts & sidewalks in Cabbagetown times when I ever was
there sweet David met Sirdaddy who gave him a pair of sky-high

red plastic platforms but he never wore them cause he'd heard Sir-
daddy'd do that for all the boys he liked & one summer we dipped

drenched to the Masquerade runoffed the black tinderbox propped
on stilts how it ground in my teen dream tongue out sizzle second

I saw him no shirt & reached his face minnows swum in through
separate sensors sensing each other & we turned what a long way

we'll never be ones for the crowd but in acts of faith & from across
the river of sound the kingdom called we both heard bells & that

tremor droning furnace cinders we're hammered in the heat can't
feel (we're so far off) you come down you burn up & get added on

Self-Portrait as St. Peter's Youth Group Member

If I ever learned   a thing   to read a text   I should say
it was   there   in the   church with chains   suspended
as   spare vertebrae   saurian nave   I was   leader

of the acolytes   would wear hair   straight as   gold
fit for goats   and people looking for   angels   with
crushing repetition   memory garden   feeble   effort

That was when   I   used to sing   lark lightly   if I ever
learned   anything   was it holding   the book   both-handed
for the gospel   at the center   for to be spoken

to the chignoned ladies   to be counted on sitting
that original comfort   But I rebelled & not   I wanted
stationed   behind the organ   thinking priestly

under my white robe   ill-fitting garment   body tampered
down   I had my   own followers   didn't quite know it
how I walked myself   alb & cinctured   so steadily

proud crucifer   before the service   Wednesday service
parsing gospel service   lock-in   under the foosball
table service   getting fiery   loving my youth leader

like a sister service   who never pressed me   to love
anything just let me   grow scales   & act wild
learning   to read   see that greater unknown & I wanted

them all   to swallow me   into the pine-nave   all the
thinkers thinking   all the repeaters repeating   when I
let myself   anemone   devouring   all the   being seen

all that   easy existing   all the kind kind snow-haired
Romans   who are all now so   long gone   as any action
I thought   the service ended   when I walked out

Lux Aurumque

The light we made
between   each other
                gravity shone
through   fifty high
school singers
                our choir

reeding pure
the grace note's
call   the dissonance
between us wrapped
our vocal folds   our
                shimmering

each word   a gold slip
                in pitches
refracted
threaded   triads
lips shaped by each
other's echo's kiss
                octaves in
staircases   warm
                heavy falling

listen   a molten song
undulating in the night
                would come for her
in wreck   in dissonance
                My mouth flew
open   no ocean's
                    mussel shell

I heard no sound of mine

but in the choral
form we held   each time
we sang   that glowing
inverted light   we recast
her shape in sound

You're Called by the Same Sound

shift of cool as you slip the nightgown over your head

mirror collection of sounds I answer

slick glove of a pond dive goldeneyed

straight arrow plunge to the soppy weed roots

we're diving down at the call of it

made present in usage practice longing for her

water furl rushes from girl knees gliding

ambience turning in time to oxbow

you and I don't touch but held in waves just past

held in thought breath never extinguishes

two lives linked in air in sound

which one of us a tuning fork I can't answer

I Wouldn't Mind Dying

Naked as a two-lane road

The traced-edge waves of foothills

In the valley of dry bones

Like a scimitar following

One point to another openly

I asked I can't remember if

We ever kissed he answered

How could you forget the field

Ice pressing my homecoming

Dress the dark his moving liplines

By and by it occurs

The unanswerable test

In my thirtieth year

I heard the storm of faces

Alone   voices singing exponential

A wheel in the middle of the wheel

The turkey vulture opens its tipped

White mouth no song comes out

We Are Always Both in the Field

Mentioning the furthest back field
a horseless space, and houseless, a
field above the aisles of daffodils in
which I once thought I'd marry—to
mention the field framed by blackberry
bushes is a curb in the mouth, a fence
pinning the swath of the field like a sheet
stretched over a face swept under
the field like a wash of a heavy
ocean, mention a wave, ask of the back
field, she will tell you of the quartz
and arrowheads—the hafted points of
clear stone found the field rising
full of all the arrowheads ever picked
up from it are told and found again
in mentioning the field, the aching
acreage accruing age, I'm chasing
away the back of the back fields waving
when I say back field I want to promise
you that I did once want to marry there
and every time I say it I hear her say
it and it's hers

Eclogue in Rills, 1944

In the spectral light of poolwater, I find her. Wearing a red swim costume.

Girl still, soft jawed, six years before her daughter.

Floating in the glorified swimming hole.

Thirty years of photographs and he appears just twice. Sidelong watching her
watch a pony's

Muzzle in her palm.

His hair already white.

He whose occipital crested the pool's surface like a turtle shell.

He who she'd drag to the shore like a log.

I have been looking for so long. Had not noticed him not there.

She came home to be married. Turned away from school, sixteen. To him.

Found herself waiting in the walled-in water.

Took her place. At the juncture.

What I can channel. Her eyes are closed, centering the pool.

If I mentioned cottonmouths she'd stop still. They nested in the pool

And so in it I never swam.

I am showing what I have of interior space, lit in memory and streaming.

I cry at the mention of snakes. Will not swim in the ocean. Do you see
me now?

So still in wading it's like air.

Dovetailing when I hear our name in the remembered pond together.

Newts, their yellow efts. So undisturbed I lift dozens up like pebbles.

Distal, girl distilled. Spectral, water. She forgets the camera was there.

Holding the Line

Through the winter I walked
from the stone house to the river,
knowing only some of purplish berries'
names...must be beautyberry, I'd note
while treading down the hill,
slick on the hill but for patches of inch-
high moss, little firs, their luminous
light-thatched green, their starcup
bristles—that's when I look for what's
intricate rather than let my sense
lead me afield...the fact is I have
to reconcile
myself if I want to go farther than
I have...to poetry's status as many
things...how far can I go? And yet
still come back?
Bootslip, stormfelled pines, I could
stop again over the broken glass edging
thru the clay—that'd be one
way, to think over liquid partitions...
lodged in a hillside—in cascade's progress
they appear, prongs, ephemera,
as though these angles have no master...
Fingerless gloves
& the globes of rain droplets orbing
from the red berries, not holly—hard—
I find to think of meaning, its source, hard
& round, water spilling over my fingertip—
I touch it, ruin it...
Watersoft, a walk to the river.
How far does this stretch, I think while
lines nearly edge through,

pitiful volunteers, impressions shading
forward—tan pine needles lining
a path taken nearly every day as
long as I can stand the cold...I lap
the field's counter where the ground goes
marsh, depression
...how to reconcile
parts to poetry I could not feel: the first
time I found the grey fur, then the
orange webbing trailing thirty coiled
feet behind, snagged,
coyote's paw cinched...puffed, newly
abandoned. I'd heard mewling at night
but mistook it
death calls...
In so listening for notes of my own
I'd misapprehended the real sound.
I thought of the coyote and thought
fur, bowed-back neck, sink
of muscle...I watched, noted it becoming
bone...I walked thru the blackberry brambles'
frosted arc
on Christmas Eve morning, and
I did not lie down with it, I did not lie
yet though I longed to...whatever
meaning may be I wouldn't make it,
not there,
even as the king snake, usually underground,
slipped past my hand resting on the wet
leaves watching the riverwater move over
the weir,
even as poetry like the water kept

a low current...
The last midafternoon I stood in a gaze
at the overlook, having forgotten myself
  nearly still,
    in a stretch of seconds the shepherd mix
following the incoming truck crept
    around the bend   it fixed upon me
stepping low, lower in crouch, lowering
    its dead eyes—my thigh—
          The man waited seconds, then called
his dog off, he waited as animal
  fear filled me, his whistle as master...
thought of a torn leg, the dog's jerking mouth...
  I walked back up to the pink sky, early
fleabane catching my eye, the house
  obscured on the ridge, a thistle, as though
                                        a flower might cohere...

I Won't Write You a Country Poem

I'm feeling low and unforgiving.
A scorpion hangs from the hook
of its tail, a long spider-web spindle
swinging in the window. I won't
have me believing in images. It swings
in the heat, heat radiating off a red
tin roof. Rising Fawn in summer, a real
place. I have split my shaded heart
in two. The cabin with a red tin roof.
Eagles, *whoop-de-doo,* curve updrafts
of ridge heat, the air over the valley
west. Actually that's a pretty big
scorpion, dangling there. Twists,
shows off its lightness. Half a finger.
If you've seen The Hanged Man, perhaps
like me, you forget that he's suspended
alive in his image's stasis, as, it
turns out, this whopper guy curls up,
skittering its six legs to no useful effect.
The spine only arcs so far backward.
Its pinchers' little lethal lines. For scale,
I introduce the cows' lowing and, no
joke, the white farmhouse in the haze
of a particulate-saturated atmosphere.
I've really been white-knuckling it just
to stay this still. Just to stay alive. And if
I'm mean enough, I'll reach up 'n' snip
the setting that ties me to this frame.
How's that freedom feel? A quick
cut cutting the quick of the heart,
that old chestnut, oh this old thing,
which reaches out, can't quite make
the cut in this life, if you will. I won't.

May Death Come Swift and Merciful

for Philip Cooper Wright, 1988–2021

Still I have not found the route to you

Running down the hard grey beach I turned

Stranded by the railroad track you sought

In the summerset aegis of proximal love

Fillialy warbling under the magnolia

I kissed your startled sister's brow like you

Through my lips my body funereal

Having dreams in the precognitive way

I once awoke knowing the pit of an action

A hole of having happened while I slept

Your head struck the ground, giddy

Your head where next you'd shoot

Thirteen years later with no signal

Those last words I sent you took

To the temple, in the fluorescence, I saw

As blood filled temporal impact's gap

As blood fills the vessels of recognition

I spoke the future ever out of grasp

You heard the sound of my voice ethering

I knew which language would reach you

A body so alike it can't be touched

Sotto Voce, Abandoned Barn

What eaves know, host
to swallow's nest,
a rat snake's ribbing wrap.
That thinking
is like that. Pine planked. Grey honeycomb

pining for originary use. Alfalfa tang,
an in-mind stench. Mind abandoned
roadside. Left like a mine

falling in. From the highest angle nests
the densest dark, riding weather

like a carriage to the ground. Tucked
in cedar, orange froth
circling nail heads. Falling
out. That thought, gripped between
my teeth and hammer claw's
the prayer
I will not say's been prayer
all the while I've been living
here. Do not labor with your prayer
like a hammer. The barn's
a colony of wood dissolving
in the dark.

Chimney

Pale pink
bricktall
it stripped
no wood or
outer frame

how I
cackle when
you wink
say *de-briss*
of debris

fire striking
the person
aglow by
the fire out
side it

the chimney
calumny
I drive by
as close as
I'll come

Bare in night
fall you know
what they say
no house so
no home

Subject Matter Comes Winging Toward Them

after William Christenberry's *Palmist Building with Camera,*
Havana Junction, Alabama, 1980

A cell, a small box
& breadth

In the light cast
on its chosen substance,
    others begin to glow

like a tripod silver
  stake marking grass
height & depth
            if that's clear

We verge to a point
Patches grassless sparse
  green frame

Is that a rangefinder
  or a window   & in it
a grid gives balance

What the frame holds
Is it a house we can walk in

A looker looking a hand
downward   Is it backward
frontside or otherwise to be
            looking like that

Is that a tree of heaven
its compound spill of leaves

a netting fringe drawing
             the sideboards back in
the thicket is
           no sacred grove

We can tell you what
is leaving   color, order drained
             did you just
structure your sight

You're Called by the Same Sound

Not the sound itself at night
but the absence of knowing
the body denying its image
whose dark-shrouded opening
become imminent ambience
sonic movement through air
brings its form to you as form
as idea neither face for memory
nor fact but the hole in the face
for the call to emit through
the darkness between leaves
fog's deposits slick and waxy
a cloud lowered to the ground
like sound it reaches you
history's muted anacrusis
the call whose source obscured
inverted breath of wail or light
bramble netted radiating clear
silence but for itself incipient
disapparition which touches
sense before its pulse

*

Honey in the Rock

What's good
  in the mouth
a cording trill

Can't you
  see all what's been

lost has did
  for me

if you hear then
you
can go

I believe her—
drank the
  living fountain

chime's the pitch
              and pluck
bliss
the perfect
  worker ever

amber

O taste and see
      blood
flood cover

Notes

p. 6: "Cloud of Unknowing"

Italicized phrases are taken from Sally Mann's introduction to her photography book *Deep South.*

p. 20: "Sotweed Factor Danse Macabre"

"Invisible angels" is a phrase from Susan Howe.

p. 22: "Aceldama"

I first learned of this place name through transcribing besmilr brigham's long, unpublished epic poem "Birth." It refers to the plot of land that Judas bought with the money he received for betraying Jesus.

Additionally, this poem takes language from *The Life and Times of Elder Rueben Ross* (1882) by his son James Ross, quoted in an article from the Southeastern Grasslands Institute, "Six Good Clues That a Southeastern Grassland Was Here." Ross was a traveling preacher, and this passage describes riding through the "Pennyroyal Plain Prairie of southern Kentucky and northern Tennessee in 1812."

p. 26: "Surveyor: John Seaborn, 1831"

Mention of John Seaborn and his dog Bruno appears in Lucy Josephine Cunyus's *History of Bartow County, Georgia, Formerly Cass* (Greenville: Southern Historical Press, 2001), 8-9.

p. 36: "Everything That Rises"

In addition to referencing Flannery O'Connor, this poem contains lines, numbers, and entries from *The Encyclopedia of Southern Culture* (1989), a refrain from Walter Benjamin's "Theses on the Philosophy of History" (1940), Edward L. Baptist's *The Half That Has Never Been Told: Slavery and the Marking of American Capitalism* (2014), Jean Toomer's *Cane* (1923), and George Herbert's "Superliminare" (1633).

p. 38: "Requiem with Flamingo Flock"

"a disturbance of words within words that is a field" is a line from Robert Duncan.

"And just on the horizon there was this huge line of pink" is a direct quotation by the scientist Pete Frezza from the NPR article "Florida's Long-Lost Wild Flamingos Were Hiding in Plain Sight."

p. 51: "Hot Blast Furnace"

This poem addresses in part the processes of the Etowah Iron Works, in operation from 1842–1864.

"Fetid scorching breath" is from Robert Hayden's "The Middle Passage."

p. 64: "Lux Aurumque"

This poem shares its title with a choral arrangement by Eric Whitacre performed by the Darlington School Concert Choir directed by Dan Bishop.

The lines "My mouth flew/open   no ocean's/mussel shell" reference Charley Jordan's blues song "Keep It Clean," additionally covered by Willie Watson.

p. 82: "Subject Matter Comes Winging Towards Them"

"In the light cast on its chosen substance, others begin to glow" and "the thicket is no sacred grove" are lines from Theodor Adorno.

p. 87: "Honey in the Rock"

This poem was written while listening to Blind Mamie Forehand's "Honey in the Rock" on repeat for several hours, and its lines reference her phrasings.

Acknowledgments

The Account: A Journal of Poetry, Prose, and Thought: "Compress Pastoral," "Buckshot," "Irradiation"

Action, Spectacle: "Subject Matter Comes Winging Towards Them," "Human Bone, Worn Lyre"

The Boiler: "Town Under Lake"

Chicago Review: "Hot Blast Furnace"

Crazyhorse: "Wraparound," "Eclogue in Rills, 1944"

Cream City Review: "In My Father's House There Are Many Houses," "Undated Incidents Concerning Occupation"

Ecotone: "Eclogue with Daylilies," "Photograph: Alice Allgood Cooper on Her Wedding Trip, 1888, " "Cotton Block"

Flag + Void: "Honey in the Rock"

The Greensboro Review: "Removal Fort"

jubilat: "Eulogy at Headwaters"

Kenyon Review: "Holding the Line," "Eclipse"

The Literary Review: "Origin Story"

Luigi Ten: "Aceldama" and "May Death Come Swift and Merciful"

mercury firs: "I Wouldn't Mind Dying"

New South: "We Are Always Both in the Field"

The Paris Review: "Everything That Rises"

Peripheries: "Surveyor, John Seaborn, 1831"

Poetry Northwest: "Night Habit," "You're Called By The Same Sound"

Prelude: "Sotweed Factor Danse Macabre"

Rampage Party Press: "You're Called By the Same Sound"

Scalawag: "Never Lived in the City," "Okefenokee"

Send Me Press: "Chimney"

The Southeast Review: "Self-Portrait as St. Peter's Youth Group Member"

Southern Humanities Review: "Cloud of Unknowing"

Sycamore Review: "Jane in Starving Time"

Tinderbox Poetry Journal: "Sotto Voce, Abandoned Barn"

Third Coast: "I Won't Write You a Country Poem"

Tyger Quarterly: "Historical Eye"

West Branch: "Requiem with Flamingo Flock"
Yalobusha Review: "Lux Aurumque"

Additional thanks to Poetry Daily for featuring "Night Habit."
"Eclogue with Daylilies" was anthologized in *The Orison Anthology* 2018.
"Eulogy at Headwaters" is anthologized in Broken Sleep's *New Ecopoetry Anthology 2022.*

My deepest regard for those whose histories I have lived alongside, and on whose thresholds I have stood with respectful intention as I've written descriptions of real historical events, sourced from both archive and folklore, and tied inexorably to place. No amount of justice can ever correct all the harm my forebears have caused, but I stand beside you now in the work towards liberation, reparation, and environmental restoration.

This book is dedicated in memory of my father, Barry Wright III. Without his preservation of our family's archive, now housed at the University of Georgia, or his own love of literature, I would not have had a place to begin. Thank you to my mother, Jacquelyn, for your unfailing belief in me.

Thank you to Mary Szybist, Bin Ramke, Elizabeth Willis, Mark Levine, Graham Foust, Brenda Shaughnessy, Robyn Schiff, and Brian Blanchfield. Thank you to Vievee Francis for a conversation asking me to be sure I could articulate what matters most in "Surveyor: John Seaborn, 1831" and by extension, the broader work of these poems. I also wish to thank Melian Radu, Ryan Tucker, Liam O'Brien, Kelly Krumrie, Emily Bark Brown, Sara McGuirk, Emily Barton Altman, Alyssa Perry, Justin Cox, Alicia Mountain, Cass Eddington, Khadijah Queen, Sara Gilmore, Timmy Straw, and Ryan Skrabalak for their direct support of this work, as well as the editors of the literary journals in which these poems appeared, particularly Anna Lena Phillips Bell, Rose McLarney, and Craig Morgan Teicher, whose early encouragement meant very much to me, and S. Yarberry, Kate Gibbel, and Ian U Lockaby for their invitations to be part of their publications. Thank you to Henry Goldkamp and The Splice Reading Series in New Orleans, and to Katie Naughton and Allyson Paty for their generosity in our writing group. To anyone who has had a critique of or kind word for these poems, or for me as this collection sought publication: thank you.

I am grateful to Shane McCrae for selecting "Jane in Starving Time" as the winner of *Sycamore Review*'s 2017 Wabash Prize, and to Roger Reeves, who selected "We Are Always Both in the Field" as the winner of *New South*'s 2015 New Writing Contest. Although I had to withdraw it from publication in the volume, I also wish to thank Brian Teare for selecting "Everything That Rises" for *Best New Poets 2020*.

"We Are Always Both in the Field" was originally for Adam, and now it is also for my father.

My utmost thanks to Kylan Rice and Lindsey Webb for believing in this book, creating the space in the world for it with Thirdhand, and for encouraging me to inhabit a fuller range of poetic accountability.

Thank you to Jonathan, my partner in world-making, in our own language.

Alicia Wright is originally from Rome, Georgia, and has received fellowships from the Iowa Writers' Workshop and the University of Denver. She is the editor of *Annulet* and publisher of Annulet Editions and works as Managing Editor of *The Iowa Review.*